WHEN
THE WOMAN
YOU LOVE
IS AN ALCOHOLIC

Joan Curlee-Salisbury

☝ **W9-AVX-348**

ABBEY PRESS
St. Meinrad, Indiana 47577

Second Printing, 1981

PHOTO CREDITS: R. Weaver, Cover; Wallowitch, Content
Photos

Library of Congress Catalog Card Number:
78-73017
ISBN: 0-87029-143-2

CONTENTS

CHAPTER ONE: Who Is an Alcoholic?

What image does the word "alcoholic" bring to your mind? Perhaps your first thought is of the classic skid-row bum, in and out of jail, sleeping in missions or doorways, begging for enough money for a bottle of wine. Or perhaps you think of a rich, happy-go-lucky playboy, who periodically checks into a plush "drying out" institution. Or of a famous writer or actor whose monumental binges get wide newspaper coverage. Whatever version of "alcoholic" comes to your mind, it is probably a man you think of. But alcoholism is no respecter of sex; women too can fall victim to this illness.

So think of an alcoholic woman; what image comes to mind now? Perhaps a bar girl, hustling drinks from the male patrons?

Or perhaps a spoiled, bored society matron? Or a famous actress? Any of these could be alcoholic, of course, but so could many other sorts of women. Think, for example, of a teenage girl, or someone's grandmother, or the nurse at the doctor's office, or a teacher in your child's school, or the woman next door. Any one of these could be an alcoholic. The problem is becoming especially serious among teenagers, and even some preteens, who are returning from other drugs to the old standby, alcohol, and are having trouble with it.

Sometimes the "typical" woman alcoholic is described as a bored suburban housewife. Again, this is just one group among many who have trouble with alcohol. The fact is, there is no typical alcoholic woman any more than there is a typical alcoholic man. Alcoholics can be found among school children and among the retired. They can be found in any socioeconomic group and any race. They may be intelligent, retarded, or anywhere in between. They may be of any religion or of none. And one of these women may be someone you love—a daughter, a mother, a sister, a wife. It is never easy to accept alcoholism in a loved one, and it seems especially hard to accept in a woman. "Alcoholism" still has some connotations of weakness or sin, despite increased public understanding that it is an illness. When it hits home in someone you love, it's hard to avoid responding emotionally with anger or denial or to resist moralizing. Even when the head knows it's an illness, the emotions may find the facts difficult to accept. It somehow seems shameful to see your wife or your mother with the same illness that afflicts the wino on skid row. But it is just the presence of this response that makes it important for you to learn as much about the illness of alcoholism as you can. If you understand, it will be easier for you to accept.

It is probably because most people think first of men when they think of alcoholism that the problem is so often undetected in women. Even physicians often overlook or misinterpret symptoms in women that would quickly lead them to suspect alcoholism in men. But in recent years there has come to be an increasing awareness of the seriousness and prevalence of alcoholism among women. In 1978, for example, the National Institute of Alcohol Abuse and Alcoholism designated women as one of its target groups for special attention, both for research and for treatment efforts. The National Council on Alcoholism, a voluntary group devoted to informing the public about alcohol problems, has formed a special women's task force.

Why all the increased attention to women with drinking problems? Perhaps it is because workers in the field are becoming aware that there are many more such women than they thought, and that their needs have largely gone unmet. No one knows with certainty how many alcoholics there are in the nation or how many of these are women. Estimates can only be made from the prevalence of certain diseases (such as cirrhosis of the liver) or from the number of persons presenting themselves for treatment. The most common estimate is that about 10 million Americans are alcoholics. For years writers in the field estimated that there were 5 or 6 male alcoholics for every female alcoholic. Now, the ratio given is usually much smaller. Dr. Marvin Block, a pioneer in alcoholism education and treatment, estimates that the numbers of male and female alcoholics are about equal. Other writers estimate that there are about 3 alcoholic men for every alcoholic woman.

A variety of theories has been presented to explain why the estimates of the number of women alcoholics have increased so drastically. Some opponents of recent liberalization of sex roles see the increase as a harmful by-product of "women's lib"—that women are suffering from a "man's disease" because they are deserting their traditional feminine role. Others, however, see just the opposite cause: women turn to alcohol because they are frustrated by the limitations of their traditional role. Another possible explanation must be considered: perhaps the number of women alcoholics has not increased so dramatically, but they simply are feeling more free to admit their problem and seek help as public information has decreased the stigma attached to alcoholism. The recent admission of alcoholism by several well-known women is evidence of the greater openness about the problem in recent years. There is some indication, however, that there are in fact more women with drinking problems now than in the past (although the increase has probably been much less dramatic than the sensationalists would have us believe) simply because more women are drinking now. The greatest increase documented so far has been among young women. In some studies of high school students, for example, the number of girls who say they drink at least occasionally is about the same as the number of boys who drink. In studies only 10 or 15 years ago, the percentages were quite different between the two groups. Not all students who drink will become alcoholics, of course, but if percentages of social drinkers who become alcoholics remain constant, this increase in the number of drinkers would inevitably increase the number of alcoholics.

If you are worried about the drinking of a woman you love, it is important for you to know as much about alcoholism as you can, and especially about some special ways it affects women. If you know about alcoholism it will be easier for you to recognize some of the behaviors you have worried about as symptoms of the illness. Some of these symptoms may be less devastating for you if your information has made them predictable. One of the hardest things about loving an alcoholic is never knowing what might happen next. The more information you have, the greater your chances of knowing what to expect, to understand what is happening, and to respond appropriately.

As social drinking among women becomes ever more common, it is difficult to distinguish normal from abnormal drinking, especially in the earlier stages of the problem. Certain symptoms have long been considered classic diagnostic signs. "Blackouts," for example, may occur once in a while for a social drinker, but rarely are common except among alcoholics. During a "blackout" a person seems to be functioning fairly normally, but afterward is unable to remember that period of time. This could be quite bewildering, for example, for a husband trying to discuss events of the night before with his wife, only to find she has no recollection of those events.

An even more clear-cut sign of the illness is the loss of control phenomenon: the person cannot be sure, once having started drinking, when he/she will stop. This does not mean that the individual will drink excessively every time he/she drinks—it just means the matter is unpredictable. A woman may drink appropriately on most occasions, but cannot be sure when she will exceed those limits—and it might happen at the worst possible time. Other so-called "classic" signs, such as tremors ("the shakes") or morning drinking may or may not be present.

Actually, almost all of the symptoms of alcoholism might be absent in a particular drinker and he/she would still be an alcoholic. The most useful definition is that a person can be considered an alcoholic if drinking is causing a continuing problem in any important area of his/her life—family, health, work, self-respect, or any other area. The key word in this definition is "continuing." If a normal drinker finds, for example, that drinking is causing conflict with her husband, she will be able to change her drinking behavior with no particular effort. If she can't, she is saying by her actions (though probably not in words) that her drinking is more important to her than marital harmony. If she is beginning to feel guilty about her drinking behavior but can't change it, she is showing that alcohol is playing a more central role in her life than her self-respect. This central role of alcohol in a person's life is a much better indicator of alcoholism than any of the traditional "symptoms."

Notice that alcoholism has been repeatedly referred to as an illness. Both the American Medical Association and the American Psychiatric Association define alcoholism as a definite disease entity. Often we think of disease only as something caused by a germ, but this, of course, is far too narrow a concept. Alcoholism is a disease in the sense that it has definite symptoms and a definite course of progression. It is not just a bad habit or a sin. No one chooses to be an alcoholic and rarely can anyone rid themselves of the illness without some sort of help. Unfortunately, many alcoholics suffer agonizing guilt because they think they *should* be able just to use their will power and stop drinking. But this is about as logical as thinking they should be able to use their will power to cure heart disease or diabetes. An alcoholic is not a "bad" person; he or she is a sick person.

The description of alcoholism given so far would apply equally to men or to women. Yet there is evidence that the illness does affect women in some special ways. The general public, for example, often views alcoholic women as somehow more degraded than their male counterparts. The old double standard of conduct for men and women has by no means disappeared, and there still is a lingering feeling that women should be more respectable, more conforming, than men. Because the role of woman has for so long been equated with the stabilizing functions of wife and mother, the drunken woman has seemed to pose a special threat. Traditionally, a husband might stray from acceptable behavior and people would expect the wife somehow to maintain a semblance of stability in the home. If the wife is showing deviant behavior, however, there is far less expectation that the husband should, or would be able to, maintain stability. Even among alcoholic women themselves it is not unusual to hear the comment, "there's nothing as disgusting as a drunk woman." According to the stereotype, a woman who has deserted her feminine role sufficiently to be an alcoholic has deserted respectability in all areas, especially the sexual ones. Students of the problem realize that this stereotype is as false as most others, yet it persists. Because alcoholic women are part of their society and were brought up with these same attitudes and beliefs, they are likely to share this feeling that they are somehow especially evil or degraded. Tremendous guilt and self-loathing are almost inevitable results.

A much higher incidence of depression has been found among female alcoholics than among male alcoholics. This is, in part perhaps, a cause for her drinking: she may be trying to "medicate" away her depression. A vicious cycle is thus set in motion: as she finds herself drinking to the degree that the guilt and self-loathing described above come into existence, she is inevitably more depressed. Thus the depression often noted among alcoholic women may be both a cause and a result of the illness. A woman could hardly avoid being depressed if she felt she was somehow a disgrace to herself, her family, and everyone important to her. She probably feels she should stop drinking and the fact that she doesn't indicates somehow that she is weak and evil. While men alcoholics have some of this same guilt and depression, it seems more severe in women because of their own awareness of, and acceptance of, society's double standard.

In a study of patients at an alcoholism treatment center, a much higher percentage

of the women patients than of the men had experienced psychiatric hospitalization. Such studies have led some students of alcoholism to the conclusion that women alcoholics are psychologically "sicker" than the men. However, this particular study was conducted in a center whose patients were primarily middle or upper class. In this socioeconomic group it was probably more "respectable" for a woman to be admitted for psychiatric treatment than specifically for alcoholism, so no real conclusions can be drawn about the degree of psychiatric illness.

There is reason to believe that men and women drink excessively for different reasons. One alcoholism expert contended that men may drink to overcome the "taboo on tenderness," a taboo that does not exist for women, who are expected to manifest tenderness. Another study contended that men drink in order to feel more powerful. A related study, using the same methods of investigation, found that women drink in order to feel more "feminine." (Just what was meant by "feminine" was not really important; the women drank to experience whatever *they* considered feminine feelings to be.)

It also has been noted that alcoholism in women is more often related to a particular situation or stress than is the case for men. Men may simply drift into alcoholism for no apparent reason from normal or socially acceptable drinking. Women more often can give a specific reason for turning to alcohol, and family members will frequently agree that the heavy drinking did, in fact, coincide with the event or situation the alcoholic woman cites. Once a woman begins excessive drinking, her symptoms are often "telescoped," that is, she may pass quite rapidly from very early indicators of alcoholism to symptoms of a very advanced stage. It is not uncommon for a woman's alcoholism to progress in 3 or 4 years to a point men may not reach until after 15 or 20 years of heavy drinking.

The problem may be complicated by the frequency with which physicians treat the symptoms of alcoholism as merely signs that the woman is neurotic and prescribe tranquilizers. Although no exact figures are available, most experts agree that far more women than men become dependent on both tranquilizers and alcohol, a potentially deadly combination. The theory behind such medication usage involves the idea that alcoholic drinking is simply a secondary symptom, a response to some underlying psychological problem, and that easing the problem with pills will take away the need to drink. It seems logical, but it rarely works. Alcoholism is an illness in its own right, a true addiction, and medicating away some degree of depression or anxiety simply does not remove the alcoholism. When pills don't provide the same feeling as alcohol, the tendency is to revert to alcohol, but often without discontinuing the pills. This more complicated chemical dependency can be extremely difficult to treat. A woman finds it hard to see that she needs to eliminate "nerve pills" as well as alcohol because, after all, "my doctor prescribed them." In one study at an alcoholism treatment center, more than twice as many women as men used tranquilizers or sedatives, and more than twice as many women were judged by their own doctors or the center staff to have problems with these medications, such as exceeding the prescribed dosage, feeling dependent on the drugs, or experiencing withdrawal symptoms when they were discontinued.

Although it was noted earlier that alcoholism can strike anyone, there are some groups of women who appear to be higher risks than others. Single women, for example, whether never married, divorced, or widowed, experience some special stresses that they may try to avoid by drinking. If you think about it, you probably will agree that our society doesn't really have much place in it for single women. Couples invite other couples to social events. A single man is often considered a real "catch" for a party, but rarely is this the case for an unattached woman. And how many jokes about "old maids" have you heard? Perhaps not as many as in past years, but they certainly still pop up. Since a single woman doesn't fit into any of the established social constellations, it can be very difficult for her to become socially involved and find the self-acceptance that would enable her to avoid, or recover from, alcoholism. She is probably holding down a job and maintaining a household—with or without children—and the effort to fulfill both the breadwinner and the homemaker roles, without anyone around to help or support her, can be terribly draining. It's easy to say, "I need a drink to calm down" or "to pick me up" or "to help me sleep." Loneliness can be especially devastating for the single woman, and it's terribly tempting to try to escape this loneliness by drinking. Sometimes her life will not seem worth the effort it is demanding. When she feels she has to escape the pressures, the bottle is a handy way to do it. For a woman who is living alone it is easier to hide excessive drinking than for a woman living with a husband or other loved one—there's nobody around to know how much she's drinking. And it may seem to her that nobody would care anyway.

Women who are seriously pursuing a career, whether married or single, also have some special pressures, especially if they are competing in fields that have been traditionally dominated by men. Despite improvement in recent years in sexist attitudes in employment, a woman who is highly achievement oriented may still feel she has to prove to men "anything you can do, I can do better." This may include feeling she has to prove she can "drink like a man," and may lead to an increased risk of alcoholism.

Others who run a high risk are those

whose husbands are so [...]
ed that all their dedic[...]
jobs, and they fail to pr[...]
support their wives need[...]
ample, leave the rearing[...]
most exclusively to the[...]
participate in family act[...]
woman in this situatio[...]
think of herself as no[...]
household drudge, and [...]
A special subgroup of t[...]
may be those who sacrif[...]
cations to help put thei[...]
school and now feel left[...]
cation and accomplishn[...]
common, for example, f[...]
out of college to help he[...]
law school, medical sch[...]
ate program and then [...]
lack of education among[...]
they begin to move. Un[...]
especially sensitive and [...]
contribute to this sense[...]
the wife may try to avoid[...]
cessive drinking.

One distinct group [...]
are those who have been[...]
riencing the "empty-nes[...]
are women who through[...]
have defined themselve[...]
wife" or "Sally's mother[...]
dividuals in their own [...]
definitions somehow change, they find it
hard to know just who they are. The woman
whose whole life revolved around her chil-

19

dren, perhaps in a way that was rewarding and satisfying for her, experiences a special emptiness when the last child leaves home. The woman who has always identified herself in terms of her husband faces serious problems if her marital situation is abruptly changed, perhaps through divorce or death. Identity problems are difficult at any age, but can be particularly devastating in middle age when a woman suddenly loses what may have been a rather comfortable and satisfying view of herself in relation to others. When these women turn to drinking, the illness often progresses very rapidly. It is possible that investigators, who have stressed the "telescoping" of women's alcoholism symptoms into a much briefer period than is usually seen in men, were seeing many of the women in this particular group. However, among other groups of women alcoholics, serious symptoms still appear more rapidly than among men, although the progression may not be so startling. But since these women feel themselves so useless and their lives so empty, it is likely that their drinking contains a self-destructive element. Karl Menninger, one of America's leading psychiatrists, has stressed this element in all alcoholism, and it is probably nowhere more clearly demonstrated than in these despondent middle-aged women.

Another group, which has only recently received attention, is found among the elderly. This could be partly a result of changing attitudes that have made drinking more acceptable among women of all ages. But whatever the reason, a number of older women—retired, widowed, perhaps feeling useless—seem to be turning to excessive drinking. American society is generally youth oriented, and has provided little real role for the elderly. American women live longer than men, creating a considerable group of elderly women who have outlived their husbands and, in many cases, their sense of usefulness. Older women may well feel the same emptiness and lack of purpose described in the middle-aged "empty-nest" group. Sometimes when the children or friends of an elderly woman learn that she is drinking too much the response is, "What difference does it make at her age? Let her have her pleasures." This response, however, misses the fact that drinking is *not* a pleasure for an alcoholic, but a necessity. It also misses some particular complications that can occur from heavy drinking among the elderly. It can aggravate health problems, for example, that may already be quite serious. It can hasten mental decline. It can damage self-respect, especially in an older woman who grew up in a generation that was even more horrified than ours at the sight of a drunken woman. It can lead to falls and other accidents, already a serious risk factor for the elderly. Note, of course, that I am not talking about the woman who sips sherry at bedtime to help her sleep or might drink a highball to stimulate her appetite. I am talking about a woman who drinks alcoholically, by the same standards that apply to people in other age groups. An elderly woman may not drink as much as a younger one, because it may not take as much to achieve the same effect. But the test is still the same: is drinking causing a continuing problem in any important area of her life?

Finally, mention must be made of women whose own alcoholism is closely related to that of someone she loves, especially her husband's. Sometimes wives become so despondent and helpless because of the husband's alcoholism that they decide to drink, too. Sometimes this begins as an effort to punish the alcoholic husband or shame him into quitting, but often it is simply an effort to escape intolerable emotions. A wife in this situation, however, may find her own drinking is out of control, doubly complicating the home situation. Women in this group have an especially hard time recovering unless their husbands, too, begin to recover. This situation is even tougher on children than having one alcoholic parent.

From this list of "high-risk" women, it may seem that virtually any woman who drinks runs a high risk of becoming an alcoholic. While it is true that many women are included in these groups, there are some common themes. All somehow have lost (or never had) a sense of identity and self-worth and have failed to learn effective ways of coping with stress, depression, and other uncomfortable emotions. All somehow are failing to find the emotional support they need. The description of these various groups was designed to help you avoid overlooking alcoholism in someone you might consider an improbable victim. If you consider the variety of women who are vulnerable to this problem, you may see it sooner and respond more appropriately.

One point needs to be stressed again: alcoholism is an illness. It can happen in the best of families—families like yours. And it is nothing to be ashamed of. Alcoholics are likely to do many things that are difficult for those around them to accept, but remembering that these actions are symptoms of an illness rather than things they choose to do may make them a bit easier to tolerate. Irresponsible or inconsiderate actions are never easy for others to accept. Some of the things an alcoholic woman will do will seem to be things that she could control if she just tried, but she can't. She probably feels as badly about her behavior as those around her—or worse. If you can remember that her actions are part of her illness, it may be easier to keep loving her even when her actions are far from lovable. You can love a person even while hating some of her behavior. It's a bit like the old saying, "God loves a sinner while hating his sin." Reminding yourself that alcoholism is an illness may make it easier to keep loving an alcoholic, whether she's your wife, your daughter, your mother, or anyone else who matters to you and deeply needs your love.

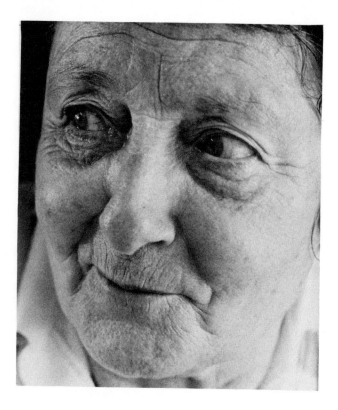

CHAPTER TWO: The Problem of Denial

It is hard to accept the fact that someone you love is an alcoholic. In fact, this can be as hard for family members as for the alcoholic herself. And just as alcoholic women feel a special shame and guilt, members of her family also suffer these feelings even more sharply than the family of an alcoholic man.

Parents of an alcoholic teenager or young adult woman may wonder how they went wrong. Where did they fail their daughter? This feeling of failure can easily turn to anger: "Why is she doing this to us?" In fact, no one knows why one person becomes an alcoholic and another doesn't, and there is no way parents can insure that their daughter won't develop the illness.

The problem of denial is especially serious in the context of a marriage. A housewife, for example, can often hide her drinking problem more easily than someone who is in the work force. She may be able to get her husband off to work in the morning and her children off to school with no signs of anything out of the ordinary. But once they are gone, she may have a day of privacy for her drinking. If her husband comes home to find her asleep, or the house uncared for, or no preparations for dinner, he may decide she's just a sloppy housekeeper and raise hell with her about it. But he's unlikely to guess that she has spent the day drinking and has made a heroic effort to pull herself together and seem reasonably sober by the time he gets home. Unless he has some special reason to suspect a drinking problem, it just isn't likely to come to mind quickly or easily, as it might to the wife of an alcoholic man. After all, he is part of a society that defines alcoholism, even today, as a "man's illness." He may admit that she is not functioning well or seems moody or irritable. In that case, he may insist that she see a doctor.

Unfortunately, doctors can become drawn into the circle of denial. All too often, if a woman complains of insomnia, "nerves," depression, or family problems, her physician may prescribe mood-changing medication without thinking to inquire about her drinking habits. Physicians sometimes say they are reluctant to ask a woman about her drinking for fear of insulting her. "She wouldn't tell me the truth if she really does drink too much," they sometimes say. "She'd just change doctors." While this may sometimes be true, physicians who have developed the habit of asking about a patient's drinking—even if the patient is a woman— have found that their patients often seem relieved to have a chance to talk about their problems. And increasingly, physicians are becoming aware of the danger of prescribing mood-altering drugs—especially tranquilizers—for people whom they suspect may be heavy drinkers. But it still happens too often—especially with women.

If a husband doesn't understand his alcoholic wife's behavior, and if her doctor doesn't find anything physically wrong, affection may fade rapidly. A husband who is angry over his wife's behavior will rarely show much sexual interest except perhaps in a perfunctory manner that is likely to provide little real satisfaction for either partner. He is likely to react to his wife's failures with anger. It is difficult for him to accept the fact that she is not simply unwilling to do her share in the marriage, but is unable to do so because of a genuine illness. He may respond with angry accusations and demands that she do better. He may respond with physical abuse. We often think of battered wives as being married to alcoholics. A husband who doesn't understand his wife's alcoholism may be so angry and frustrated by her behavior that he responds with vio-

27

lence. Whether the abuse is verbal or physical, it can only lead his wife to more drinking as she feels even more guilt and shame complicated by a sense of rejection and failure as a wife.

Even when her drinking problem becomes obvious, her husband may try to explain it away or pretend it doesn't exist. He may insist that she could stop if she only would. It is at about this stage that the alcoholic woman may begin to hear, "If you loved me, you wouldn't drink." He may insist she use willpower or "take the pledge." He may plead with her to stop, or threaten to leave her. All these approaches make about as much sense as begging her not to have diabetes, or saying she wouldn't have heart disease if she really loved him. But all too many husbands still respond to a wife's drinking as if it were a moral issue, or a matter of choice, rather than a serious illness.

When he finally realizes that all his threats and moralizing will not stop her drinking, he may begin to protect her. He may start to make excuses for her, to himself, to their friends, and to the children. Social life is often curtailed because he cannot be sure she will be sober enough not to embarrass him. He becomes reluctant to invite anyone to the home because of her unpredictable condition, and finds reasons to refuse invitations for the same reason. As social life is curtailed and other activities are eliminated, the couple is thrown together more and more exclusively and a climate for ever greater resentment and anger is created. And this climate contributes to more drinking rather than less, as the wife tries to escape intolerable emotions.

Often the entire family becomes isolated and shut off from activities that once were important to them. The children fear inviting their friends into the home because they don't want anyone to know their mother is a drunk. They may find themselves, too, making excuses for their mother, especially to themselves. It is never easy to fully accept the fact that a woman you love is an alcoholic. Family members may find it easier, for example, even to believe that she is mentally ill than that she is alcoholic. Somehow it seems more acceptable for your wife or mother to "have a nervous breakdown" than to have the illness of alcoholism.

Although other family members contribute to this deadly denial, it is usually the husband who plays the game most vigorously. If he admits the seriousness of his wife's drinking problem, it somehow reflects on his ability to control her. Men often feel that their wives are drinking simply as a form of rebellion and that if they, the husbands, were as strong and dominant as they "should" be, they would be able to stop their wives' drinking. Along with the anger that the apparent rebellion creates, guilt usually begins to emerge. The husband may feel that he is somehow responsible for her drinking—that he is somehow the cause and therefore should be able to correct the problem. Even the children sometimes get caught up in this sense of guilt: that somehow they must have failed their mother if she found it necessary to turn to the bottle. But as so often is the case, guilt and anger go hand in hand. If an alcoholic makes you feel guilty, which is a thoroughly uncomfortable feeling, it's easy to be mad at her for making you uncomfortable. None of this is very logical, of course, but a family's response to alcoholism rarely is logical. And somehow it seems even harder to be logical and appropriate when the alcoholic you love is a woman. Because of our continuing double standard of conduct for men and women, it is especially difficult and embarrassing to have an alcoholic woman in the family.

Women who are married to alcoholics often get much sympathy from friends and family. "Poor Sue, married to that no-good drunk, bravely trying to hold the family together," and on and on. But men who are married to alcoholic women rarely meet the same response. It seems somehow to reflect on his ability to choose a wife well, or gets involved in the control issue discussed already. Men who are married to alcoholics usually find it very difficult to discuss the problem with others. As a result, they have less chance to learn the facts that might make it possible for them to understand what is happening. They tend to pretend that the problem isn't there, or hope it will simply go away by itself. And meanwhile they continue to protect their wives from the consequences of her drinking. They make excuses for her, they try to take on some of her duties around the house, they defend her to children and friends. With the best of intentions, they are protecting her to death; with this much denial and protection, she is much less likely to seek and find the help that could arrest this progressive illness.

It has often been said that any family with an alcoholic member becomes a sick family. Their response to the alcoholic's drinking leads them to both devastating emotional turmoil and social maladjustment. Some experts feel this is especially true for families trying to cope with an alcoholic woman. As the family members feel anger, guilt, resentment and an entire array of other emotions toward their wife and mother, their own mental health is inevitably harmed. And as she sees her loved ones being harmed by her drinking, she is likely to feel even more evil and shameful—and helpless. She may make efforts to control her drinking, only to have them fail. She may even be able for a time to stop drinking entirely. During this time, her husband and children will probably feel deep relief that the problem has ended. But alcoholism is an illness that is marked by relapses, and permanent sobriety rarely occurs in persons who do not understand the illness and do not seek and receive some sort of help in dealing with it. So when a relapse occurs—when she starts drinking again—

31

there is a tremendous sense of disappointment in everyone concerned. The husband
is likely to feel betrayed; his wife said she
had stopped drinking and he believed her,
and got his hopes up, only to have them
dashed. This process is likely to be repeated
again and again, until he braces himself not
to dare hope. And the sad part is, his wife
probably got *her* hopes up, too, and was
even more disappointed.

As trust within the family breaks down,
communication becomes more and more
difficult. Whatever closeness may have
existed in the family tends to crumble, as
each member tries in his or her own way to
cope with feelings about the alcoholic's
drinking and her behavior while drinking.
People who drink excessively hurt those
who love them. This may seem too obvious
to mention. But a woman who hurts her husband and children while drinking suffers
tremendous remorse when she realizes what
she has done. And a natural response is for
them to react by hurting her. A pattern of
almost constant painful reactions sets in
among family members. Even the nonalcoholic members hurt each other because of
the endless tension they are experiencing.
In short, virtually every member of an alcoholic's family becomes emotionally drained.
A husband may be speaking far more
literally than he realizes when he says, "I'm
tired of your drinking." It is exhausting living in a household filled with bitterness, de-
spair, guilt, disappointment, anger, dis-

trust—all the emotions that go with living with a drinking alcoholic. But perhaps the most devastating emotion that develops in an alcoholic's household is loneliness. Both those who love her and the alcoholic herself can grow to feel that no one quite understands what they are feeling or can help them.

As family relationships break down, the husband will finally see that he can't control his wife's drinking and can no longer protect her from her drinking problem. All too often, his response to this recognition is simply to leave. Far more wives remain with alcoholic husbands than the reverse. A pattern frequently seen is for a husband to deny his wife's drinking and try to protect her and then, when he feels he can take no more, leave her and divorce her. This of course further reinforces her view of herself as a hopeless failure.

For a working woman, married or single, a similar pattern sometimes takes place. Employers or supervisors, like husbands, tend to overlook signs of alcoholism in women and then protect them, pretending the problem is not there. Their reason for this is not much different from the husband's: the stigma against alcoholism in women is simply so great that a conspiracy of silence develops. No one wants to believe or admit that "that nice lady" is an alcoholic. The pattern of protection on the job can be just as harmful as it is at home. Rather than confronting her when her drinking interferes with her work and encouraging her to seek treatment (or even insisting!), the situation is ignored until matters reach a point at which there is no choice but to fire her.

If any of these ways of relating to your alcoholic sound familiar to you, you have been responding to the illness in some of the most common, but least helpful, ways. But all these responses are perfectly natural reactions to a cunning and baffling illness. Your emotions have been involved, and you have probably been thrown off balance. Don't be too hard on yourself. You have been doing what comes naturally. But if you can see the uselessness of these reactions, even their actual harmfulness, then you can start looking for other ways to respond to the illness. Sometimes it may seem that the alcoholic's drinking has destroyed all love in the family. But it is when people do deeply love and care about each other that they hurt one another most deeply. And the love that contributed to the hurt can also be the most powerful force in gaining the strength to try other ways of dealing with the problem. And this is where recovery begins—for yourself, whether the alcoholic stops drinking or not.

CHAPTER THREE: Out of Denial

O.K. You've babied her, begged her, threatened her. You've been angry, hurt, frustrated. You've tried all the usual tactics: marking bottles so you can prove how much she drank, pouring out her liquor, withholding money. But none of it has worked. She's still drinking and the family is still obsessed by the drinking. It seems that everything in the family's life revolves around her drinking. So, where do you go from here?

Some changes will obviously have to be made. And these changes will have to be in *you*—the nonalcoholic who loves an alcoholic woman, whether you are husband, mother, sister, son, daughter, or friend. Why should *you* be the one who has to change, when you don't have the problem? Well, the reason is really simple: it is because you are the only person you *can* change. No matter how much you want to modify the alcoholic's behavior, you can't really control it, and efforts to do so only lead to frustration and increased breakdown of family life. The fact is, she has a right to make her own mistakes, and you can't prevent her. But you can keep her problem from utterly dominating the family and destroying the rest of you.

The only way you can really cope with an alcoholic in the family is by striving for some degree of detachment—by realizing that you didn't cause her drinking and can't correct it. It's tempting sometimes to wonder what you did that caused her drinking, but the fact is that no one can cause another person to drink, and no one can control another person's drinking. Remind yourself that alcoholism is a real illness, and you didn't cause it any more than you might cause diabetes. This can be a difficult fact to accept. It's easy enough to know, in your head, that you are not the cause of her alcoholism, but it's another thing to accept it in your emotions. Yet, this is where it has to be, if the knowledge is to be of any use. You have to remind yourself again and again: I'm not the cause of her drinking and I can't be the solution.

So what does this detachment involve? Well, the rest of the family can still do things together, whether the alcoholic can join them or not. If a husband and children have stopped going to church, for example,

because they're tired of making excuses for their "sick" wife and mother, they're making a mistake. They need the strength and comfort of their faith now more than ever — and they don't owe anyone an excuse if their mother isn't along. And you can accept social invitations, whether your alcoholic will be up to going or not. More of your friends than you expect will understand. In other words, the nonalcoholic members of the family have to keep living their own lives. They have to get away from being obsessed by, and controlled by, the alcoholic.

You may be surprised by how well some social gatherings will go. It isn't unusual for an alcoholic woman to say, "I can handle parties all right. I can drink soft drinks, or have a drink or two, and manage all right at a party. But then when I get home, I feel I owe myself a reward. And that's when I really get loaded." This sort of behavior is naturally bewildering to her family. In fact, her unpredictability is a big part of the reason for the family's drawing in on itself. But remember that she is a person in her own right. If she goes to a party and makes a fool of herself, that's her problem, not yours, no matter how embarrassing it may be for you. Remember: every person has a right to make his or her own mistakes—and to take the responsibility for them. But the rest of the family needs to protect itself and not stay in a shell.

But don't you care about her self-destructive behavior? Of course you do, and you try to convey this. But you also need to make it clear that the entire family isn't going to self-destruct with her. If you make this clear, in a loving way, you are really taking a tremendous load of guilt off her shoulders, a guilt which can well lead to more drinking. If a woman feels her family's life is being damaged by her drinking, she is bound to feel a great deal of remorse, and one way to avoid remorse is by drinking.

Linda, for example, is an alcoholic married to an alcoholic. Whenever she drinks, he uses it as an excuse to drink. He also has a heart problem, which makes drinking especially hazardous for him. Whenever he drinks, Linda feels such acute guilt that she is driven to try to relieve it by more drinking. And so the cycle goes on. She drinks and he retaliates by "getting drunk at her." And it hurts, so she tries to relieve the hurt by more drinking. Somehow these two need to learn that each is responsible for his or her own life, not for anyone else's—not even that of a spouse.

So what do you do to help an alcoholic woman? First of all, you learn the facts, by reading a book like this. And then you help by offering steadfast love, in any way you can. A friend may play as significant a role as a family member. Linda, for example, was deeply moved when a neighbor brought a bag of tomatoes to her home with a note reading: "We still love you. Call if you need us." Knowing that Linda and her husband probably weren't eating much while drinking, the next night the neighbor and her husband brought dinner to the house. This may seem contradictory to the idea of detachment, but it really isn't—these friends weren't trying to control, they were simply trying to show that they cared, and it came across loud and clear.

One of the best ways someone who loves an alcoholic can get help is by contacting Al-Anon, the offshoot of Alcoholics Anonymous. The Al-Anon family groups are based on the idea that family members and friends of alcoholics need help, too. Although Al-Anon has often been thought of as being primarily for wives of alcoholics, it should be made clear that it is for anyone involved in a relationship with an alcoholic. And Al-Anon *is* for men, too. In fact, in larger cities there are "stag" groups. Al-Anon is for anyone who cares about an alcoholic—husband, brother or sister, mother or father, or friend.

The main thing in going to Al-Anon is to know that you're going for yourself, not to make *her* stop drinking. As you consider the Twelve Steps—the same steps used by Alcoholics Anonymous—you will see that these steps can apply to your situation. For example, the first one while it may seem strange does apply: "Came to believe that we were powerless over alcohol—that our lives had become unmanageable." Husbands, or others close to alcoholics, sometimes say, "But I can manage alcohol. My drinking isn't out of control." But what he's missing is the idea that he can't control *her* drinking; in that sense, his life is unmanageable. And when an entire family's life revolves around whether the alcoholic is drinking, isn't that unmanageable family life? Her drinking is controlling them—they are not managing their lives in a reasonable, independent way.

In Al-Anon you will meet others who have had many of the same experiences you have had or are having, and it can be a great source of help just to know that there are others who understand, who can share their experiences with you, and who care about you. Often those who love alcoholics feel terribly alone, as if no other person could ever have experienced what they have. Just sharing experiences and feelings can be a great source of strength. And sometimes there are practical suggestions from those "who have been there." They may tell you, for example, how useless it is to pour out liquor — and the advice has special authority coming from someone who tells you he or she has tried it, and it didn't work.

Part of what you'll hear at Al-Anon involves the concept of "tough love": loving an alcoholic enough to make her pick up after her own mistakes. This can be a simple thing like letting *her* be the one to call and apologize if she failed to meet some responsibility or made a fool of herself at a party; it's her behavior, not yours, so you shouldn't be the one to apologize. If she leaves the car parked in the neighbor's yard, she should be the one to retrieve it, not you. If she can't make it to work, let *her* call the boss with an excuse.

This is clearly being "tough" but in what sense is it "love"? It's love in the sense that you are showing that you care enough to force the alcoholic to face her drinking behavior and its consequences. The more you protect her from this confrontation, the more you are playing into her denial system, and the harder you are making it for her to

41

see the need for change. The idea is that there has to be some real discomfort before a person is willing to change. Somehow the pain of present behavior has to become greater than the pain involved in risking change. This is basically what Alcoholics Anonymous describes as "hitting bottom."

When you have really accepted the idea that you cannot control her drinking and will not try to cover up or accept responsibility for her behavior, what then? Then you start rebuilding your own life. When a family is obsessed by an alcoholic's drinking, all other interests tend to be pushed aside. But now you owe it to yourself to rediscover old interests—or discover new ones. If you're a father, for example, how long has it been since you took your kids fishing or bowling? We talked earlier about how important it is for a family to return to as nearly normal a life as possible. Some of your new Al-Anon friends may be able to help by sharing how they were able to resume a normal life. Pick the winners. Listen, especially, to the Al-Anons who seem to have the quality of family life you would like to have.

In some cases, the entire family, or some part of it, may need something more. Don't hesitate to turn to professional counselling. Your clergyman may be a good place to start. An ever-increasing number of clergymen of all faiths are coming to a greater understanding of alcoholism, the illness, as opposed to drunkenness, the sin. If you have not been active in a church, inquire around about what clergy have been especially helpful in counselling alcoholics and their families. Again, Al-Anon may be a good place to start this inquiry. When a clergyman is especially effective in working with alcoholics and their families, the word gets around.

If he feels you need more help than he can give you, your clergyman may refer you for professional counselling. Don't resist this or feel embarrassed about it. Many people at one time or another find themselves in a crisis situation and need some special help. And living with an alcoholic—or even just loving one—can create an entire series of crisis situations, and at times the stress may be just too great to face alone.

Most cities, and even some smaller communities, have community mental health centers, where fees are adjusted to income. This is certainly a resource worth exploring. Some centers have staff members especially trained in family counselling. Family counselling, or family therapy, focuses specifically on the interactions within the family, rather than the problems of individual family members. In an alcoholic's family, these interactions, even among the nonalcoholic members can become disturbed, and need professional sorting out.

Remember, we're talking now about the nonalcoholic family members and how they can find the help *they* need. We're not talking about getting help to stop her drinking. Changes within the family *may* help motivate her to stop, but that's not the main focus right now. The fact is that anyone who loves an alcoholic, especially those who live with her, develop problems of their own. This applies not only to husbands and children, but to anyone who feels close to an alcoholic—parents, brothers and sisters, friends. Watching self-destruction in a loved one is never easy, especially when some of the most lovable traits may seem to be lost first. And it's easy to slip into self-pity: "Why did this have to happen to *my* wife? Or *my* daughter? Or *my* sister?" Again, the idea of detachment is vital. She became an alcoholic for reasons of her own (reasons no one is too sure about), not because of you.

Will your detachment, your "tough love," the lessons you learn at Al-Anon, your efforts to rebuild your own life, make your alcoholic loved one stop drinking? No one can predict that for sure. Evidence seems to be that these steps do help motivate change, but the most important effect is the salvaging of what has been called the "other victims"—the four or five other persons seriously affected by every alcoholic's drinking. And this is worthwhile, whatever happens to the drinking alcoholic.

CHAPTER FOUR: When There Are Children

Cindy worries about her children. "When I'm drinking, they do anything they want to do. Then when I'm sober, I try to crack down on the discipline."

Cheryl reports just the opposite pattern. "When I'm drinking I'm awfully tough on the children—no noise, full completion of jobs around the house, the whole works. Then when I'm sober, I feel ashamed of myself and pamper them, not asking much of anything from them."

Both these women have reason to worry about their children. This sort of inconsistent discipline is thought by many child psychologists to be more damaging than consistently loose or consistently severe patterns of discipline. The child is left not knowing what to expect, or what is expected.

Life for a child growing up in a home with an alcoholic is never easy, but it may be especially difficult if the alcoholic is the mother. After all, she is the one who is involved the most in early childhood rearing and continues, in most households, to be the one most involved in the child's day-to-day training. Some studies show that children of alcoholics are several times more likely to become alcoholics themselves than the children of nonalcoholics. While some interpret this as an indicator of a hereditary factor in alcoholism, it is just as easy to see it as the result of living in the disruption of a household in which one parent is alcoholic. There have been no really conclusive studies comparing the effect of an alcoholic father to that of an alcoholic mother, but impressionistic studies indicate that the children of alcoholic mothers have a tougher time than those of alcoholic fathers.

The reasons aren't hard to understand. As noted earlier, more wives stay with alcoholic husbands and try to maintain some semblance of stability in the family than when the wife is the alcoholic. Thus children of alcoholic mothers are much more likely to be left with only one parent—an alcoholic mother. Further, the children are likely to share society's view that alcoholism is somehow worse in women than men, and lose all respect for their mother.

What can be done to help these children? If the father remains in the family, and if he understands alcoholism, he can provide a real source of strength as he helps the children understand that their mother has an illness. They need to be told, lovingly and repeatedly, that their mother's actions toward them, that seem so unreasonable and even unkind, are not a reflection that she doesn't love them, but that they are related to her drinking, and that this is a matter of her being ill, not bad. They also need to be reassured that when their mother doesn't seem concerned about them or doesn't seem to understand them, this is not because of some shortcoming in the children themselves. Young children, especially tend to interpret any rejection or mistreatment as a reaction to some deficiency of their own: "If I'm not loved, it must be because I'm somehow unlovable." An understanding father can do a great deal to overcome these feelings, by showing the children that he, at least, finds them lovable and worthy of his concern. He can also help the children keep some love for their mother, even while they don't love some of what she is doing. If he himself has been able to maintain his love for their mother even while some of her actions may have been unlovable, this will be communicated to the children.

But what if the father is no longer in the family, or if he has rejected his alcoholic wife? Then others near the children may need to play the role described above. It may be a grandparent, an aunt or uncle, an older brother or sister. Anyone who under-

stands and loves the alcoholic can help her children. Especially for young children, understanding, loving family members are of first importance. But if children do not feel they can discuss their problems and feelings with a family member, then they should be urged to go to someone else—perhaps their clergyman, a favorite teacher, a counselor at school—anyone whose opinion they would value. Sometimes it's hard for a family member to realize that a child might be better

able to discuss his or her feelings with someone outside the family, but this is really not
so surprising. These people have a distance
from the problem that gives their reaction a
different "feel." Children must not be made
to feel guilty if they find it easier to talk to
someone other than a family member.

Sometimes children become protective
of their alcoholic mother to the point of
helping her deny her problem, just as her
husband may have done. Some, especially
the oldest of several, may become preco-
ciously good homemakers—cooking meals,
caring for the younger children, cleaning
the house. While it's easy to admire these
skills, persons near the family need to realize
that these kids need a chance to be kids, not
grown-ups before their time. These children
can be helped to see that they are making it
easier for their mother to avoid her responsibilities and thus making it more difficult for
her to recover.

For teenagers, the problem can be especially acute. At a time when they badly
need to be accepted by their peers, they may
feel unable to ask friends to the house
because they are ashamed of their mother's
drinking. They may feel that they can't
accept social invitations because of their
burden of caring for younger children or the
house. And at an age when rebellion is
natural, they may react in either of two
extreme ways. They may turn against their
mother and make her (and her drinking) the
explanation of all their problems. Or they

49

may turn against all those who criticized her drinking (especially their father) and become overly protective of her. As with younger children, they may blame themselves for their mother's problem and feel they should somehow be able to remedy it.

Because the problem of an alcoholic parent can be so devastating for a teenager, it is important to know that help is available. Just as Al-Anon, described earlier, is for adult family members and friends of alcoholics, there is also a related group, Alateen, designed especially for teens with an alcoholic in the family or in some other significant relationship. As in Al-Anon, the focus in Alateen is on helping the nonalcoholic family member deal with personal problems and feelings, not in making the alcoholic stop drinking. And in Alateen, too, there is a great comfort in sharing experiences with others who have gone through the same thing. A teen with an alcoholic mother may feel terribly alone and may feel that no one understands. It is a great relief to find others in the same boat and be able to discuss the situation with them.

A recent TV program, "Francesca, Baby," portrayed this matter quite poignantly, as Francesca, whose mother was alcoholic, found a new sense of fellowship and acceptance in Alateen. She also found a new detachment—a realization she wasn't the cause or cure of her mother's drinking. She had been desperately worried about her mother's smoking in bed while drinking, and had tried to police her mother on this. Finally, through Alateen, she realized she couldn't control her mother's risky behavior, so she rigged a rope ladder as a way of escape in case her mother set the house on fire. She had learned an important lesson: she could not change her mother, but she could protect herself from some of the possible ill-effects of her mother's behavior.

For anyone working with the children of alcoholics, self-preservation is the important lesson to convey. The children don't have to let their mother's drinking destroy them. This is the message of Alateen and should be the message of anyone working with an alcoholic's child, whether a teen or a younger child. Somehow this message needs to come across: you are loved, you are important, you have a life of your own that is valuable, no matter what happens with your mother's drinking. Ideally, other members of the family are key figures in getting this message across, but others—friends, teachers, anyone the child has confidence in—can also help.

The children of alcoholics seem to get into trouble more often than kids in general. This may be partly because they haven't had consistent discipline during their lifetimes, but it may be in part a way of saying, "Hey, I'm here. Look at me. Give me some attention." Even bad attention is better than none, and often an alcoholic mother can get so wrapped up in her own problem that she isn't fully aware of her children's needs, or doesn't have the resources to deal with them.

Eve, for example, was horrified to learn that her children, in their midteens, were not only smoking marijuana but were also experimenting with other drugs. When she confronted them with what she had learned, they had the perfect comeback: "What's the difference between our doing drugs and your doing booze?" She had no real answer, except that she didn't want them to have to experience the years of trouble and suffering that she had known. But it added another chunk to her already heavy load of guilt. An alcoholic mother doesn't need to be reminded that she has failed her children; she knows it already, all too well.

When Eric and Jerry were living with their alcoholic mother, they reacted very differently. Jerry, who was in high school and had always been a good student and popular in his class, started to become a withdrawn loner, and his grades dropped. Eric, in junior high, became an unmanageable hellion, shooting his pellet gun against signs and mailboxes in their apartment complex, and generally getting a reputation as a real brat that no one could do anything with. Their older sister, out of school, tried to help the boys, but their reaction toward their mother seemed too strong for her to overcome. Their grandparents, who might have helped, had steadfastly denied that their daughter had any problem. Finally, it was decided that the only solution was for them to live with their divorced father, a solution that seems to be working out well. They see their mother on weekends, but are freed from the day-to-day stress of coping with her drinking and unpredictable behavior.

Sometimes this solution, getting children out of a home headed by an alcoholic mother, may be the only way out. But in many other cases, probably most, some loving intervention can keep the home together. In the case of Eric and Jerry, for example, if there had been someone to reinforce the messages their sister was trying to give them—that their mother was sick, that they were important and loved—it might have been enough. But she had no one to turn to for help. The job was just too big for a young girl alone.

So what can be done for these youngsters? Most of all, someone who cares about the children of an alcoholic mother has to show love and concern. Somehow they need to know that someone understands how tough things are for them, and that someone cares. They need a chance to learn the facts about alcoholism, so that perhaps they can come to know that their mother is ill, not unloving or "bad," and that her situation is not something they need to be ashamed of.

CHAPTER FIVE: When She Wants Help

Sometime or other the woman alcoholic you love will decide she wants to stop drinking. In Alcoholics Anonymous the expression used is that she "hits bottom"—reaches a point at which the pain of drinking outweighs the rewards. This does not mean that she has had to lose everything, but just that drinking no longer offers enough gratification to offset the difficulties it causes. The family or other loved ones can help bring about this decision-point. Even though she knows she needs to stop drinking and really wants to, at least intellectually, there is likely to be some ambivalence. Her loved ones can help weight the scales toward sobriety by confronting her with the problems her drinking has caused. In a calm, loving way all the members of her family and perhaps friends as well can simply present facts—not recriminations—and let the evidence build up enough that she is forced out of her denial.

Sue, for example, finally began taking steps toward sobriety when her husband gave her examples of times when his business relationships were damaged by her behavior; when her daughter explained why she never invited friends to her home because of times when her mother had embarrassed her; her neighbor reminded her of the time she knocked over his mailbox; her clergyman told her of the times her behavior had been inappropriate at church meetings. She had been able to minimize all these things individually, but when she was forced to look at them all at the same time the evidence was overwhelming that she did in fact have a major problem—she could not ignore it any longer. This loving confrontation should be calm, factual, and specific if it is to be effective. If it turns into an emotional harangue, she is more likely to become defensive than convinced.

If she is employed, her supervisor may play a key role in this confrontation. In this case, as with friends and loved ones, it is important that the material she is forced to face be factual and specific, and presented in a calm manner. She may be tempted to say that her private life is none of her boss' concern, but she can hardly say that if the supervisor presents specific situations in which her work was impaired because of her drinking. He might, for example, point to a record of excessive absenteeism. He might give her evidence of declining efficiency.

If, as a result of this confrontation, she decides she is ready to "do something" about her drinking, then you can be supportive in helping her find sources of treatment. Often, even when an alcoholic wants to stop drinking, he or she does not know how to do it or where to look for help. You can be ready to provide this information when the time comes.

A starting place should be your family physician. When a person has been drinking heavily over a considerable period of time, only a physician can determine whether she can safely stop drinking without medical supervision. Alcoholic withdrawal symptoms are no joke, and not just a matter of minor discomfort, but can be quite serious. Her doctor can decide just how much medical help she needs in withdrawing. Although prescribing tranquilizers over a long period is harmful for an alcoholic, these medications do have a valid place in easing withdrawal, and her doctor may want to use them. Remember, though, that they are useful only over a short period of time while she is trying to get off the booze, not over the long haul as a substitute for the alcohol. She may need vitamins, as well, or other medical treatment. While drinking she has likely avoided her doctor, so a complete physical probably is in order.

The doctor may decide that she needs a period of hospitalization. Most general hospitals now accept, on the same basis as any other patients, those with a diagnosis of alcoholism. In fact, any hospital that gets any federal funds (and this includes almost all hospitals) is required by federal law to treat alcoholics. Hospital treatment may ease the difficulties of withdrawal, but it is only the beginning of real treatment. When she is released from the hospital she is "dry" but still a long way from real recovery.

It may be that her doctor, the alcoholic herself, and you will agree that she needs a longer period of treatment in a specialized alcoholic treatment center. There are a number of these throughout the country, and probably one near you. Most communities will have several sources of information about what treatment center is available where, and can probably also provide information about the type of treatment delivered, average length of stay, and cost. If your city has an affiliate of the National Council on Alcoholism, that would be an excellent source of information. Your doctor or clergyman may know a treatment center to especially recommend. All the states have alcoholism agencies, and a call to the local office can get the information you need. A community mental health center may be a good source of information. If you have been involved with Al-Anon, ask your Al-Anon friends for recommendations. They probably know which centers have been successful and which ones haven't.

Alcoholism treatment centers typically are residential settings, where one should expect to stay from two to five or six weeks. During this time, she will be given a chance to evaluate her own situation and make some positive plans for maintaining sobriety. Although simply having several weeks in a setting that is alcohol free may be helpful, this is a minor part of the program at the really effective treatment centers. The main emphasis is on learning how to live an alcohol-free life. Many treatment centers utilize group therapy as well as individual counselling in an effort to help an alcoholic determine just what her problem areas, her strengths, her priorities, may be. The goal is that she will come out of treatment with a real desire to stay sober because she can see something else in her life that she wants more than she wants to drink.

Many treatment programs include sessions for family members. If the program your loved one is in has some special offering for family members, participate fully. You need this understanding, as well as needing to know how to help her. You need to know how to handle your own feelings, your own uncertainties, your own resentments, and your frustrations when she doesn't do what you think she should. One of the main frustrations for people trying to treat women alcoholics is often the unwillingness of their family members to participate in programs planned for them; wives of male alcoholics usually attend regularly, but husbands or other loved ones of the women are much less likely to become a real part of the treatment process.

Either her doctor or the staff of a residential treatment program may prescribe Antabuse as a part of her treatment. This is a drug that does nothing—unless she drinks while taking it. It is not a mood-changing drug, like the tranquilizers, and does nothing to alleviate any "craving" for alcohol. But if she is taking it, she knows she will become violently ill if she drinks. The Antabuse-alcohol reaction is rarely dangerous, but quite uncomfortable. At the first drink of alcohol, she will begin to feel flushed, and will develop a pounding headache. Her heart will seem to be racing, and she may have a sensation of difficulty in breathing. In short, every body function seems speeded up. And somewhere along the line, violent nausea and vomiting will probably start. Then the reverse of the "speeding up" sets in, and everything seems to slow down. She will become clammy and feel weak. Persons describing this experience often use the words, "I thought I was dying."

Antabuse is no cure-all for alcoholism, but it can be helpful in buying time for an alcoholic to learn ways, other than drinking, to deal with her problems. If a person has been taking Antabuse regularly, she may get a reaction if she takes a drink as much as a week or ten days after the last dose she took. Knowing this, when considering a drink, she has to stop and consider the danger of an alcohol-Antabuse reaction, and probably will elect to avoid the alcohol until it is "safe." Chances are very good that if she waits five to seven days she will overcome the mood that made drinking a probability, and perhaps will get back on the Antabuse instead of alcohol.

Whether or not an alcoholic needs hospital treatment, a main source of continuing help is Alcoholics Anonymous. This is a fellowship of men and women who share their experience of overcoming drinking problems. While most people think of AA simply in terms of a member calling another when tempted to take a drink, the program is really much deeper than this. Alcoholics Anonymous provides a chance for an alcoholic to make new friends—nondrinking friends. It also encourages her to look at herself honestly, to see her strong points and her weaknesses, and to discuss this personal inventory with some other person.

The program stresses the importance of turning one's life over to a Higher Power— "God, as we understood Him." There is nothing doctrinaire in AA—whichever God, or a Higher Power, has meaning for an individual is sufficient. The point is that the person recognizes that there is something bigger than herself in the universe, and becomes willing to let this Higher Power control her life.

When an alcoholic is drinking, she may

feel that no one could possibly understand or accept her. Within AA, she finds others who can truly understand, because they have had similar experiences. She can find the sort of warm acceptance necessary for the rebuilding of her self-respect, which probably is badly battered in the early days of her sobriety. She can learn new problem-solving techniques by sharing her difficulties with other members and hearing how they handled similar problems. She will find an abundance of inspiring role models— people who had problems as bad as hers, but now are sober. They provide her with constant proof that it can be done. And just as important as the fact that these people are sober is that they are happy about it. There is nothing grim or gloomy about an AA meeting. In fact, newcomers and visitors are often impressed by the amount of laughter they hear. "How can they joke about such a tragic subject?" is a frequent question. But they can joke about it because they're free. They have been through the valley and come out on the other side. It is rare to find any group of people who express true fellowship as completely as these people who have shared a common illness and are now bound together in common recovery.

After she has been in AA for some time, she may be asked to help out a newcomer. This "Twelfth Step" work is an important part of the recovery process. It is an important contribution to anyone's self-esteem to become part of the solution rather than part of the problem. Everybody needs to be needed. Working with a newer member also bolsters her determination to stay sober; she knows she would be letting down someone else as well as herself if she drinks again.

Alcoholics Anonymous teaches that total abstinence is the only way to avoid reverting to all the problems associated with alcoholism. Members learn that they have a chronic, permanent illness and can never return to normal social drinking. But if a member does take a drink ("has a slip"), she will be warmly welcomed back when she is ready to stop again. No one points fingers. Instead, they'll say, "I know I'm just one drink away from a drunk myself." No one in AA will say, "I'm never going to drink again." Instead, the motto is, "One day at a time—just don't drink today."

Although there are many routes to becoming sober, AA seems to have the most to offer in terms of helping the individual remain sober and live a happy, constructive life. Alcoholics Anonymous is available almost everywhere; just check your telephone directory. And it is free; there are no dues or fees. If your town is too small to have a group meeting, you can almost certainly find AA by going to a nearby town that is a little larger.

It may be that she will need some psychotherapy, as well as AA or other specific treatment for her alcoholism. This does not need to be an "either-or" decision. There is no reason why several treatment modalities

63

cannot be used together, and many alcoholics find a combination approach more helpful than any one alone. She may, for example, take Antabuse, attend AA and also see a
mental health professional for help with
some of the problems of living. Many alcoholics lose some of their problem-solving
skills while drinking and need help in re-
gaining them. They probably have problems with self-esteem and professional help
can be valuable in dealing with this. Many
women alcoholics, especially, have problems
with depression and may need help on this
particular problem. You can ask your own
doctor to recommend someone in the mental
health field or, if you have a community
mental health center, that may be a place to
find the proper helping person. Remember,
it is no disgrace to need the help of a psychi-
atrist, psychologist, or social worker. Many
people have problems that they need help in
solving.

Marital problems may remain large
enough that counselling will be required.
Here, again, call your community mental
health center or your local mental health association to find out what is available.
Especially in larger cities, you may find such
a resource as couples' group therapy. You
may be surprised at what is available even in
some smaller places. Don't be afraid to ask.
You may find that family therapy, including
the children and any members of the ex-
tended family who may be on the scene,
would be helpful, especially if the breach be-

tween mother and children is pronounced, or if communication within the family has broken down significantly.

Whichever direction you decide to go, enter into the process wholeheartedly. While it is true that basically her drinking is her problem and she has to solve it for herself, your active participation can make things much easier for her and greatly enhance the chance of success. You have an interest in her recovery, too. After all, your life will be more pleasant if the woman alcoholic that you love finds successful treatment.

CHAPTER SIX: Road to Recovery

Martha thoroughly enjoys Alcoholics Anonymous, and finds it a great help in maintaining her sobriety. She would like to attend several meetings a week. But her husband objects, so she is limited to one each week. He was happy when she stopped drinking, and encouraged her to attend AA for the first few months. But after that, he felt the problem was licked, and that her obligation was for her to be with him in the evenings, not at "those meetings you don't need any more." He wants her to keep him company, to entertain their friends, to go places with him, as if the drinking problem had never existed. He feels she is "well" now, and can return to normal living patterns.

What he doesn't realize is that she is suffering from a chronic, life-long illness and will always need to devote much of her attention to her own recovery. Members of Alcoholics Anonymous rarely refer to themselves as "recovered alcoholics"; it is much more common to hear them describe themselves as "recover*ing* alcoholics, sober today by the grace of God and Alcoholics Anonymous." The recovery process is a life-long process of growth, not something one accomplishes once, for all time. During her drinking period, the recovering alcoholic lost out on many problem-solving skills that she will need to learn or relearn. Her self-esteem has been badly damaged and won't be restored in a few weeks or even a few months. Real recovery takes time, and a great deal of support from those closest to her. She will need much support and encouragement, and often this is hard to get from those who think that physical sobriety marks the real solution to her problems. Actually, becoming physically sober is only the beginning of the recovery process that can enable her to grow and to genuinely recover from the disease of alcoholism.

The children of alcoholics often have an especially hard time accepting the idea that their mother still has to work actively at sobriety, even though she is no longer drinking. They may feel a need for additional affection to make up, in some sense, for what they feel they lost while she was drinking. One alcoholic described an evening when

her four year old, far too young to understand the complexities of the problem,
climbed onto her lap and asked, "Why do
you have to go to those meetings?" After
much thought, her mother answered, "Because I love you." And this is in fact why she
may need to spend many evenings away
from her family—because she loves them
enough to put a very high priority on maintaining her sobriety.

In Alcoholics Anonymous, one may
often hear, "This is a selfish program, and
you have to take care of yourself first." This
may sound strange, in the context of a program based on helping others, but actually
it is simply a practical statement. If one cannot do whatever is necessary to keep him- or
herself sober, he or she cannot be of any
help to anyone else. This is something that
must be remembered within a family as
well: your loved one will have nothing to
give you if she returns to drinking, so she
must do whatever seems necessary to stay
sober, even if it sometimes seems to interfere
with normal family life.

One way, of course, that you can
minimize this interference is to become
involved yourself. If you were in Al-Anon
while she was drinking and in the early days
of her sobriety, by all means stay active.
Having a nondrinking alcoholic in the family requires many adjustments from everyone involved. Others who have had to face
these same adjustments can be helpful to
you. You continue to need peer support and

69

advice just as much as she does. The entire dynamic of family life is changed when a member stops drinking alcoholically. How do you reintegrate into the family's life the person you have felt it necessary to exclude from many things because of her drinking? How soon do you let her take more financial responsibility than you could allow her while drinking? How do you help the children resolve their very mixed feelings? How do you get over your own resentments? These, among many others, are questions Al-Anon can help you resolve. Just as the alcoholic never outgrows her need for Alcoholics Anonymous, you never outgrow your need for Al-Anon.

When she was seeking sobriety, she may have sought some form of psychotherapy. Sometimes those close to an alcoholic, especially husbands or parents, may feel that once she is sober she no longer needs this sort of treatment. The truth is, however, that if she has some real underlying problems, these can be dealt with effectively only after she is sober. It is virtually impossible to do anything much more than crisis intervention with an alcoholic who is drinking. The time for dealing with her real conflicts or personality difficulties is after she is sober. In fact, many therapists will not work with an alcoholic who is still drinking, since they feel she cannot adequately understand her difficulties when the relief of drinking is so readily available. So you can help by encouraging her in any sort of on-going treatment that will help her understand and accept herself. You can help her see that she still has problems with which she may need help, even though she is not drinking. All her problems will not just vanish when she stops drinking. She may still need help with problem-solving techniques and self-understanding even when she is not drinking—or especially when she is not drinking.

Similarly, if you have been involved in family or couple therapy, you may find that it is only after she has obtained some period of sobriety that you will begin really to hit pay dirt. An alcoholic's drinking can provide a powerful smoke screen, and everything wrong in a marriage or parent-child relationship can be blamed on it. In fact, however, the situation may be, and probably is, much more complex, and only after the drinking is out of the way can these complexities be resolved. It's easy, but not necessarily accurate, to blame everything on the alcoholic's drinking. You—the husband, son or daughter, parent, or other loved one—may need to make some changes, too, if the family is to succeed. Only after she has obtained a period of sobriety can this smoke screen be lifted enough for you to assess the changes you may need to make. And there probably are some. Family conflicts are rarely the responsibility of one member alone, no matter how sick that member may be.

But what about the day-to-day functioning of the family? Can you let her resume normal responsibilities? It probably is best to do so, as an expression of trust, if nothing else. But don't be surprised if she sometimes goofs. It's hard to relearn some of the habits of normal functioning and she'll make mistakes. So don't expect too much, too fast. Accept her mistakes. After all, don't we all make them? If she is blamed, on the basis of her alcoholism, for every mistake she makes, it can only increase her sense of guilt and inadequacy, and increase the chance that she will return to drinking. She will have some relearning to do, especially if her drinking continued over a period of years. Be patient.

The major message for those who love an alcoholic, especially in the early days of her sobriety, is to be patient. She will make mistakes. Some of them may be the same mistakes she would have made if she had never had a drinking problem, and some may be directly related to her misperceptions because of her drinking. But be patient. Give her time to find herself again. Accept her limitations and failures just as you would if they had not been in any way related to drinking. After all, everyone has a right to be wrong, sometime, don't they?

Most of all, a recovering alcoholic needs a loving, supportive environment. She needs to know that people really care about her, and value her, as a person, regardless of what she has done in the past. She needs to know that the people close to her believe in her and feel she can succeed in overcoming her alcoholism. She needs to be surrounded by people who care, who will accept her shortcomings while she learns, or relearns, ways to cope with problems. She needs people who will support her as she struggles to again be a capable, contributing part of her family rather than "the family problem."

One of the problems faced by loved ones of alcoholics is trying to gauge just how careful they need to be of her feelings. When a woman is newly sober, those around her may tend to walk on egg shells, trying to avoid upsetting her. This may be a valuable attitude for a while, but soon it becomes demeaning; you are treating her as less than a fully mature human being. Most of us don't expect others to go to extremes to protect our feelings, and neither should she. We are, in fact, contributing to her sense of being something special, or someone especially vulnerable, if we don't react to her much as we would to anyone else. If she's acting bitchy, tell her so. If she's showing excessive self-pity, let her know it. If there's a valid difference of opinion, go on and argue. It's an insult if you don't—you're saying, in effect, that she's too fragile for you even to disagree with. Some arguments are natural in any intimate relationship. You are respecting her as a valid, mature part of that relationship when you go ahead and argue. You can't protect her from all challenges and frustrations, and you are expressing your confidence in her as a person when you don't try to protect her. But be patient when

73

her reactions aren't entirely appropriate, just as you would be if she had never had a drinking problem. Don't blame all her shortcomings on her drinking. This is very unfair, for the same failures could have been there without a drinking problem.

Above all, it is important not to throw up her drinking to her as the cause of all family problems, all her personal problems, all your problems, all the children's problems. She probably has enough feeling that this might be the case. It is especially tempting when angry to say something like, "Oh, if you hadn't been such a damned drunk everything would have been all right." But this sort of accusation can accomplish nothing except to make her feel badly enough to resume drinking.

When the alcoholic woman you love is trying to recover, she may be irritable and often react in negative ways. But this is true of anyone recovering from a chronic illness. You, as the loving and supposedly healthy person, may need to show a lot of patience and tolerance. You need to help her build her self-confidence, her self-esteem. These have taken a terrible beating during her drinking. To know that someone believes in her and trusts her can be tremendously important.

You may help her by encouraging her to resume community activities. She may, for example, have dropped out of church activities. You can help her get back into the mainstream of things. Help her know that you want her to participate in activities that are important to you. If other members of the family have gone to church while she was too drunk to go, let her know that you welcome her participation. Encourage your clergyman to give her this message, too.

In short, you need to show her that you value her and you trust her. She needs your love and support, not your condemnation. When the woman you love is an alcoholic, it isn't easy for anyone—not for you, not for her. She loves you and wants to please you, yet because of her illness she knows she can't. But your continuing, loving support can make a great difference in whether she recovers, or doesn't. If you stand by her and believe in her, her chances of recovery are much greater than if you reject her. She needs you—whether husband, parent, child, or friend—if she is to recover from a potentially fatal disease, alcoholism. For in the final analysis, recovery consists of getting greater gratification from people than from a chemical.

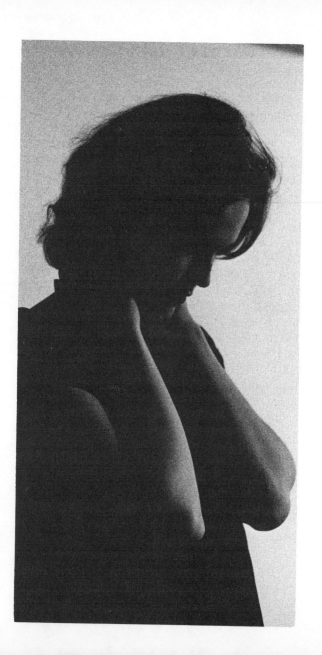

CHAPTER SEVEN: Special Problems

Drinking and Pregnancy

In 1968, Dr. Pierre Lemoine of Nantes, France, described a number of disorders that occurred among the children of alcoholic women. This report was largely unnoticed, however. Earlier comments on the effects of maternal drinking on offspring had come to be disregarded as nonscientific or the result of outmoded ideas. In 1972, however, Dr. Christine Ulleland of Seattle, Washington, noted that children of alcoholic women tended to have growth deficiencies and to lag developmentally. In the very brief period since these first reports, a definite pattern of abnormalities has been noted, now called the Fetal Alcohol Syndrome. Cases have been detected in virtually every U.S. city as well as in Canada, England, Germany and Switzerland. This pattern of abnormalities, once thought to be quite rare, now is seen as the second or third most prevalent cause of mental retardation. And the tragedy is that it is completely preventable.

Although many organs may be affected as part of the Fetal Alcohol Syndrome, its major impact is in growth deficiency. These babies are generally well below average in birth length as well as birth weight (although their birth weight is not abnormal for their length, as would be expected from malnutrition). Their heads tend to be small even for their reduced length, and their eyes are undersized. The midface may be small, giving a relatively flat appearance to the face. Some show heart abnormalities or malformation of the limbs.

The most striking and tragic aspect of the Fetal Alcohol Syndrome is mental retardation, ranging from profound retardation to almost normal (a few children showing some aspects of this syndrome are of normal intelligence). Apparently the effect of alcohol on the developing fetus' brain goes beyond generalized intelligence. These children have often been described as "jittery" or "restless" as newborns, and many have behavioral problems and poor coordination as they get older.

Postnatally, the babies continue to grow at a slow pace, and may become underweight for their length, even though their weight to length ratio was normal at birth. The rate of growth in length is about two-thirds that of the normal rate, and weight gain may be only half the normal rate. Although there has been some evidence that deprivation or neglect were involved if the children remained with their alcoholic mothers, there has been no indication that these deficiencies clear up when the babies are in good foster homes or even in a hospital. There are only a few reports of improved brain growth, even among the children in good environments. The IQ usually does not improve with age; although one study reports a few significant increases in IQ, it also reports some significant decreases in other children, while most remained approximately the same over several tests. The evidence, then, is that this syndrome is not reversible. Even with the best of care, these children will remain handicapped people.

Much remains to be learned about the type of drinking that results in these serious problems. One study which involved 41 infants in Seattle, Washington, showed that what the mother drank seemed to have no effect on the prevalence of the Fetal Alcohol Syndrome. Affected children were found among women drinking primarily wine, gin, vodka, bourbon, or beer. Many of the women who produced children with the Fetal Alcohol Syndrome drank heavily throughout their pregnancies. Little is

79

known about the possible effects of occasional binge drinking or whether there are some periods in the pregnancy when the fetus is especially vulnerable to the effects of alcohol.

There appear to be some ethnic differences in the frequency rate of the Fetal Alcohol Syndrome. The University of Washington researchers, for example, found highest frequency among American Indians, then Blacks and Whites, in that order. These differences may reflect differences in the frequency of chronic alcoholism among women of reproductive years in these groups.

Spontaneous abortion is more frequent in chronically alcoholic mothers, suggesting that alcohol, in excess, may actually be deadly to the fetus. One study, for example, reported a seriously affected child whose alcoholic mother had seven successive miscarriages prior to the pregnancy with the affected child.

Most of the early studies dealt with women who, by any standards, had severe alcohol problems. But what of the moderate drinker? Or the woman who may be toward the heavy end of the social drinker spectrum? What of the woman who usually drinks moderately, perhaps often abstains completely, but who once in a while drinks to intoxication? Although there is not yet any conclusive evidence linking light to moderate social drinking to the Fetal Alcohol Syndrome, estimates of the amount of alcohol necessary to cause damage seem consistently to be going down. The evidence that even moderate drinking during pregnancy can cause some degree of impairment has led the National Council on Alcoholism to urge complete abstinence during pregnancy. Certainly some women, perhaps most, can drink moderately with no ill effect on their babies. Even among chronically alcoholic mothers, many of their children appear normal in both growth and function. One estimate, however, is that the Fetal Alcohol Syndrome appears in some 33% of the offspring of severely alcoholic women and that mental deficiency, to some degree, is found in about 50%. Even if the numbers prove to be lower, this still represents a significant number of impaired children, who will remain impaired as adults. Even a tiny number is too many, when the condition is completely preventable.

So what do you do when an alcoholic woman you love becomes pregnant? First of all, you can provide her with information about the dangers to the unborn baby. Although there have been TV programs on the subject, newspaper and magazine articles about it, etc., there are still many women who are not aware of the problem or of its severity. You—whether a husband, parent, friend, or any other concerned person—can at least provide a warning. Physicians, especially gynecologists and obstetricians, can be a major source of this vital information. Prenatal clinics can also provide the needed warnings. But the people nearest the woman can probably be the most helpful, especially if they provide the information factually and calmly rather than as nagging.

Some women, even those with severe alcohol problems, are able to greatly decrease their alcohol consumption or even abstain during pregnancy if they are really convinced that drinking might harm their baby. The fear of harming the unborn child can in some cases provide the motivation necessary for the pregnant woman to seek treatment, whether through AA or through some form of outpatient or residential treatment. If she seems to be considering such a step, those nearest to her can help her make the decision. A warm, supportive manner in assisting her is essential; a nagging, preaching, name-calling approach can only lead to negative reactions and perhaps a rejection of the very suggestions she was wanting to hear.

For a woman with more moderate drinking habits, abstinence during pregnancy may be fairly easy. Some women find the physiological effects of alcohol unpleasant during pregnancy, and this, coupled with fear for the safety of the baby, may make abstinence an easy choice. If, despite her knowledge of possible harm to her baby, she finds it difficult to stop drinking, or to keep it very minimal (perhaps one or two drinks occasionally), she may find that it is time to examine her drinking habits and discover whether her drinking plays a more central part in her life than she had previously realized. This may be a good time to test how dependent she may have become on alcohol.

Despite his worry about the effects of her drinking on their offspring, her husband or boyfriend cannot control her drinking. He can encourage her to stop, help her find sources of help, and assure her that her sobriety (and the well-being of their baby) are important to him. He must accept the fact, however, that in the final analysis her drinking is her own responsibility and not his.

Teenage Drinking and the Prevention of Alcohol Abuse and Alcoholism

Anyone who has seen the devastation drinking can cause in the life of a woman he or she loves is inevitably concerned about forming healthy drinking habits in the young girls in his or her life. These concerned people may be the girl's parents, grandparents, sisters or brothers, friends, clergyman, teachers, or anyone else in a position to help her form her attitudes. As pointed out earlier, there has been a significant rise in the percentage of young people who drink, and this rise has been especially striking among young girls.

Although the exact reasons for this increase are not clear, a number of possible explanations have been offered. For one

83

thing, teenagers today have more money and are more mobile, thus making alcohol easier to obtain. The tremendous scare about the "new" drug scene—drugs with which parents had little experience or familiarity—may have made adolescent drinking more acceptable to adults. A school principal said recently that when he confronted parents with indications of drinking problems in their children, the most common response was: "Whew! What a relief! I was afraid you were going to tell me she was on drugs!" The truth, of course, is that a drinking adolescent *is* on a drug, and a very powerful one. But perhaps because it is legal, commonplace, and familiar, it seems less threatening to parents.

Some young people report that their first drinking experiences were at home, perhaps with parental approval. Others, however, started drinking with their peers, even in the face of parental disapproval, as a desire to be part of the group or to be grown-up or sophisticated. Young boys often brag about the amount of alcohol they consumed and how drunk they got as part of the rites of passage to adulthood. Girls, however, are more likely to want to show that they can remain in control of their drinking and not make fools of themselves. They may be using alcohol in an effort to make themselves more comfortable and thus feel more feminine and attractive, especially if they feel unsure of themselves socially. For some, drinking may be part of a generalized rebellion against parental authority. Or, as with adults, it may be a response to personal problems they have not yet learned how to handle.

Sheila was in a treatment center for alcoholism at 17. She said she began drinking in her freshman year at high school, just to be "one of the group." Soon, however, she found that drinking was more important to her than to her friends and that she was drinking because she frankly liked the way it made her feel, regardless of any social considerations. She also smoked marijuana occasionally, but when asked which she would continue to use if she had to give up one or the other she responded without hesitation: "Oh, I'd keep the booze. Pot doesn't do anywhere near as much for me!" Her drinking had reached a point where she had been placed in two foster homes and asked to leave both of them because of "unmanageable" behavior. She was in the treatment center on a court order, but seemed to be really profiting from her experience and to be determined to maintain sobriety. Only time can tell, of course.

Not all girls who drink develop such severe problems. But how can you best protect the child or adolescent you love from developing problem drinking? It is fairly well established that "scare tactics" consisting of posters, slogans, and statistics about the dangers of alcohol rarely have much effect; young people rarely see themselves in the posters or statistics. Somehow, young people, even those far below the normal drinking age, need to learn about alcohol in a factual, positive manner, in terms that will enable them to judge for themselves what is best to do. If young people are to learn either to abstain from alcohol or to drink sensibly and with restraint, much depends upon the person, or people, doing the teaching. It is futile for a parent who frequently overindulges, for example, to urge children or adolescents not to drink or to drink in moderation.

Parents who wish their children to abstain will have to be abstainers themselves; children learn much more from what they see their parents do than from what they say. A few solid facts can be presented in a way that will have meaning for young people. They need to learn, for example, that a high percentage of auto accidents and deaths, especially among the young, involve alcohol. Since driving is an important part of a young person's sense of adulthood, the dangers of mixing alcohol and driving may well make an impression when other facts would not. In addition, parents or other concerned persons need to help a girl who chooses to abstain by giving her ammunition for her resistance to the pressures of her drinking associates. She needs to develop a firm conviction that drinking is not universal and there is no disgrace in choosing to avoid it. She can, in fact, develop a sense of freedom in making her own decision on alcohol use, rather than following the pattern set by her peers. Young people need to learn to refuse alcohol without appearing sanctimonious or "holier-than-thou." If they can be matter-of-fact and nonjudgmental in refusing to drink, they will probably find that their peers can accept their decision. But somehow the persons close to a young girl or boy need to help the young person see that avoiding drinking is not embarrassing, shameful, or a sign of weakness. Drinking is not a measure of adulthood or virility. It is not an effective easer of pain or a solution to problems.

Young people who decide not to abstain can be helped to use alcohol responsibly and with relative safety. There are some differences among cultures in the way people drink and the incidence of alcoholism. Parents and others close to young people can help instill some of the attitudes and practices typical of cultures with low rates of problem drinking. Young people can learn, for example, that those who have little trouble with drinking are more likely to associate drinking with eating in a slow, relaxed manner and with the company of others. Drinking may be taken for granted with neither an overvaluation or a taboo, but persons are not admired for the amount they can drink and drunkenness is condemned. Young people can be helped to see that it is more adult and acceptable to drink for pleasure rather than to show off. Seeing "show off" drinking as "kid stuff" may be a powerful deterrent. Parents and other significant persons who drink moderately and associate drinking with companionship and food are showing their children a mature and acceptable use of alcohol. Parents who drink hastily or to intoxication, who laugh at drunkenness, or who drink too much and then drive are negating all the good lessons they may have taught young people in words.

In the final analysis, the only real way to avoid alcohol abuse is by improving a child's overall sense of worth and her sense of closeness in a warm family with sensible attitudes toward drinking. Anything which improves a girl's overall sense of worth, her ability to solve problems competently, and her sense of being loved helps inoculate her against problem drinking.

Concerns Unique to the Treatment of Women Alcoholics

Until quite recently, most treatment programs for alcoholics have been designed for men, with women added almost incidentally, on the assumption that whatever worked for men would work for women. To some extent, this assumption has been justified: many women have recovered in treatment settings developed primarily to meet the needs of men, and certainly both men and women have been successful in Alcoholics Anonymous. Some studies, however, have indicated that men and women do not respond equally well to some treatment modalities. At one treatment center, for example, men rated group experiences as much more helpful than the women did, while the women tended to feel especially helped by individual counseling contacts. Perhaps comparable recovery rates for men and women at this facility were primarily the result of the fact that both treatment modalities were available, so different patients may have responded well to different parts of the program.

Women alcoholics often suffer even more than their male counterparts from a lack of self-worth and an inability to make their own decisions. Perhaps they were reared in an environment that made the female submissive; perhaps they acquired this mind-set in the course of their developing alcoholism. Whatever the source, it is important that they find a way to value themselves and to feel that they have some options, some decisions open to themselves as persons. Many women alcoholics tend to be quite passive and, even in treatment, accept whatever decisions are made *for* them rather than insisting that they have significant input into their treatment plans.

But a woman alcoholic is still a human being. She still has choices. And she can decide what she will or will not accept in the plans that are made for her in a treatment setting. She must recognize that she has some autonomy, some freedom of choice.

In this connection, perhaps assertiveness therapy can be especially valuable. A woman who has always allowed others to make her decisions for her—her parents, her husband, her children—may find a real sense of relief in making some of her own decisions—even if they are wrong. Assertiveness training teaches a woman to make her own decisions and accept responsibility for them. She does not need to rely on someone else to decide for her. To baby her, to make her decisions for her, is to degrade her as less than a fully functioning adult, and that's not what she needs. She needs concern and patience, but not control. Some treatment centers include assertiveness training in their program, especially for women. However, if she does not find it in her treatment setting, there are a number of excellent books on the subject which she can read and apply; check the public library.

Another special problem for women alcoholics can arise from their concern for their children. Many women are reluctant to acknowledge their alcoholism and seek the treatment they need because they fear they will lose custody of their children. The husband, or ex-husband, can be especially helpful here, if he can assure his wife that he will not try to gain custody of the children if she will genuinely try to find help. In a few settings, treatment for the alcoholic woman is combined with care for her children, but these facilities are still few and far between. Certainly more are needed. Meanwhile, friends and family members by helping with child care can make it much easier for a woman to seek treatment.

Much more needs to be learned about the specific needs of women in alcoholic treatment programs. We need to learn, for example, what sort of vocational guidance is especially needed by such clients as young mothers, middle-aged women seeking to reenter the work force, or women who need careers as a source of identity. Women who are single and the sole source of support for a family have special vocational needs, needs which often are not met in treatment settings. When vocational evaluation and counseling are available, they are often geared to the needs of men, with the assumption, often unwarranted, that a woman will have someone to meet her economic needs. But considering the number of alcoholic women who are divorced or who have never been married, it becomes clear that vocational counseling is just as important for them as for men.

For example, Blanche in her 50's was in treatment for alcoholism. She had lived a comfortable, financially secure life for 32 years, as the wife of a physician. She never held a job except occasionally to help her husband in his office. When her children grew up and her drinking got out of hand, he divorced her. Now she is bitter about her situation: "What did 32 years as a doctor's wife teach me about how to make a living? Or how to live alone?" Although she is receiving excellent treatment for her drinking problem itself, no one is helping her specifically with her adjustment to the demands of her new, single life. The bitterness and frustration she feels about her new situation may well lead her to return to drinking. Although her ex-husband is providing some financial support, she feels rejected, useless and lonely, and doesn't know what to do with her time. Employment could be an important part of her total program for sobriety, but no one is helping her evaluate her potential for employment.

To say that women alcoholics have special treatment needs does not necessarily lead to the conclusion, reached by some feminists, that treatment for women needs to be carried out exclusively in all-female treatment settings, staffed entirely by women. It does mean, however, that questions need to be asked about the specific needs of women. A great deal more research will be required to determine how to tailor treatment to the needs of women. A determined effort will then have to be undertaken to meet those needs.

If you love an alcoholic woman, you probably will not be in a position to directly change treatment modalities. But you can help by making inquiries about treatment settings she may be considering, or that you may be considering recommending to her. The more you know about various programs the more helpful you can be in finding the treatment setting that will be best adapted to her specific needs.

Where to Look for Help

ORGANIZATIONS

Alcoholics Anonymous, Al-Anon, Alateen:
Check the white pages of your telephone directory. Most towns and cities have a listing at least for AA and they can tell you where to contact Al-Anon and Alateen, if they do not have separate listings. If you don't find a listing in the telephone directory, look in the newspaper classified ads, usually under "Personal." If these efforts fail, you can contact national headquarters to find a group near you:

- Alcoholics Anonymous World Services
  P.O. Box 459, Grand Central Station
  New York, New York 10017

- Al-Anon Family Group Headquarters
  (also for Alateen information)
  P.O. Box 182, Madison Square Station
  New York, New York 10010

National Council on Alcoholism:
Check your telephone directory for this, too. If you don't find a listing, contact

- National Council on Alcoholism
  733 Third Avenue
  New York, New York 10017

National Clearinghouse for Alcohol Information:
A federal government agency that can provide helpful information. Contact

- National Clearinghouse for Alcohol Information
  Box 2345
  Rockville, Maryland 20852

FURTHER READINGS

There are so many books, pamphlets, journals, etc. dealing with alcoholism that the following list makes no attempt at being inclusive. It merely suggests a few titles that might be especially helpful. Many other titles have been omitted which are equally valuable.

Alcoholics Anonymous, Al-Anon, and Ala-teen literature is available at meetings, or write to the addresses above for a price list.

Hazelden Books has a number of helpful books and pamphlets available from Box 176, Center City, Minnesota 55012. You can obtain a full catalog including prices and information about ordering by sending a card to this address. Some especially relevant titles:

Books:
- Kimball, B.J. *The Alcoholic Woman's Mad, Mad World of Denial and Mind Games.*

- McCabe, T.R. *Victims No More.*
  Stresses the entire family's need for help and understanding.

Pamphlets:
- Burgin, J.E. *Help for the Marriage Partner of an Alcoholic*
- Curlee, J. *Alcoholism and the "Empty Nest"*
- Kellermann, J.L. *A Guide for the Family of the Alcoholic*
- Kellermann, J.L. *Alcoholism: a Merry-Go-Round Named Denial*
- Kimble, B.J. *The Woman Alcoholic and Her Total Recovery Program*
- McGuire, P.C. *The Liberated Woman*
- Weinberg, J.R. *The Deadly Silence: Friendship and Drinking Problems*

Books and pamphlets from other sources: Many of these are available in public libraries and bookstores.

Burns, E. *The Late Liz*. New York: Appleton-Century Crofts, 1957.
An autobiographical novel of one woman's alcoholism and her recovery.

Department of Health, Education and Welfare. *Thinking about Drinking*. Washington, DC: Public Health Service Publication No. 1683.
Facts about alcohol prepared for young people as a basis for discussion of attitudes about drinking.

Estes, N.J. and Heinemann, M.E., eds. *Alcoholism: Development, Consequences, and Interventions*. St. Louis: C.V. Mosby Company, 1977.
A variety of topics related to alcoholism by prominent writers in the field, each writing about an area of his/her special interest and knowledge. Contains chapters on such topics as alcoholism in women, AA, Al-Anon, and the Fetal Alcohol Syndrome. Some parts of the book are technical, but most of it can be understood by anyone.

Greenblatt, M. and Schuckit, M.A., eds. *Alcohol Problems in Women and Children*. New York: Grune and Stratton, 1976.
Like the previous book, this one is by a wide variety of contributors and some of the chapters are fairly technical while others are suitable for a wide readership.

Kalant, O.J., ed. *Alcohol and Drug Problems in Women*. Toronto: Addiction Research Foundation, 1978.
Again, a book with sections of varying difficulty.

Keller, J.E. *Alcohol: A Family Affair. Help for Families in Which There Is Alcohol Misuse*. Santa Ynez, California: The Kroc Foundation, 1977.
A brief book well summarized in its subtitle.

Lindbeck, V. *The Woman Alcoholic. Public Affairs Pamphlet 529.* New York: Public Affairs Committee, 1975.
Clear and readable, meant for the general public.

Mann, M. *New Primer on Alcoholism.* New York: Holt, Rinehart and Winston, 1958.
Somewhat dated now, but still a valuable source of information, clearly and compassionately presented.

Presnall, L.F. *Search for Serenity.* Salt Lake City: Utah Alcoholism Foundation, 1959.
Although much of this book is directed toward alcoholics and their families, it provides some good mental health tips for everyone.

Rebeta-Burditt, J. *The Cracker Factory.* New York: Collier Books, 1977.
An autobiographical novel about an alcoholic woman, sometimes funny, sometimes sad, but with a definitely up-beat ending.

Robe, L.B. *Just So It's Healthy.* Minneapolis: Comp-Care Publications, 1978.
A clear, down-to-earth discussion of the Fetal Alcohol Syndrome.

Saltman, J. *The New Alcoholics: Teenagers. Public Affairs Pamphlet 499.* New York: Public Affairs Committee, 1973.
Despite the title, this pamphlet also contains valuable tips on how to help young people form attitudes that will help them avoid alcohol problems.

Sandmaier, M. *Alcohol Abuse and Women: a Guide to Getting Help.* Washington, D.C.: National Institute on Alcohol Abuse and Alcoholism, 1978.
Clearly written for the general public, an effort to understand this problem as well as suggestions about where to go for help.